For Juliet, with Love —S.L.J.

For Nick and Jon —S.H.

WALKER BOOKS
AND SUBSIDIARIES
LONDON · BOSTON · SYDNEY · AUCKLAND

First published in Great Britain 2012 by Walker Books Ltd, 87 Vauxhall Walk, London SE11 5HJ

10 9 8 7 6 5 4 3 2 1   Text © 2012 Sally Lloyd-Jones   Illustrations © 2012 Sue Heap

The right of Sally Lloyd-Jones and Sue Heap to be identified as author and illustrator respectively of this work has been asserted by them in accordance with the Copyright, Designs and Patents Act 1988

Published by arrangement with Random House Children's Books, a division of Random House, Inc. New York, New York, U.S.A.

This book has been typeset in Stempel Garamond   Printed in China

British Library Cataloguing in Publication Data:
a catalogue record for this book is available from the British Library

ISBN 978-1-4063-4004-4

www.walker.co.uk

How to get a JOB
by Me, The Boss
and Sally Lloyd-Jones
and Sue Heap

MY CHAIR

If you want to get a Job, first you need to know what exactly a Job is.

A Job is so you can have something to do
and get money for your family.

And sometimes a Job is so you can
get all dressed up and wear
your new shoes to work.

Some jobs are very BIG.
Like President of the WORLD.

Some jobs are very small.
Like Balloon Holder.
(Except sometimes your balloon can pop
and then you are Unemployed,
which means now you don't have a job.)

★ Sitting in your chair eating biscuits
(School is a sort of job because you do HOMEWORK.
Except they don't pay you ANY MONEY.)

Before you get a job,
you need to decide what you want to be
when you grow up.

You could be a Cowboy
or an Explorer
or someone who drives a Big Red Car.
Or even a Super-Ballerina-Football-Mermaid-Fairy Princess.
(Like me.)

Or actually ANYTHING you want!

Except you shouldn't be a Robber.
It's not allowed.

(Some people want to be
a Penguin when they grow up.
But that's just silly.)

A good job to get is something you love.
For instance, if you like going on tiptoes best
you could be a Ballerina.

Or if you like balls best, you could be a Football Player.
Or if you love holding your breath,
you could be a Scuba Diver.

But it must be something you're GOOD at or no one will
want you to do it for them.

Like, it's not suitable to be a World-Famous Chef if you can't even cook cereal.

Or a Hairdresser if you don't know ANY good Hairstyles.

Or a Spy if you don't know any good hiding places and you just sit there and everyone can see you.

If you are a Magician
first you have to find someone you can cut in half
who won't mind.

Then you call them "My Lovely Assistant"
and do Friendly Smiling at them
so they won't run away.

Next you get an Audience
and shout, "I will now pull a horse out of this bag,
EVERYONE!"
And then you go, "Wham! A horse! Bam!"
and a horse is there!

If you are a Doctor,
you need to get a White Coat
and some Patients.

Next you go around with a big needle
saying things like "I'm afraid it's
GANGRENE-CHICKEN-SCARLET-MUMPY-POX!"
and "We should operate IMMEDIATELY!"
and "AMPUTATE!" (which means CUT IT OFF!).

HERE'S WHAT ELSE YOU DO IF YOU'RE A DOCTOR:

Look inside patients' mouths for Germs and Tonsils

Listen with your Stethoscope

Write stuff like "Ear Infection" and "DANGEROUSLY allergic to Broccoli!" on pieces of paper and give it to them

And that's your Diagnosis (which is what's wrong, basically).

Then you write a Prescription (which is how to get better) like "The only cure is M&M's!"

And then you put plasters on and they feel better.

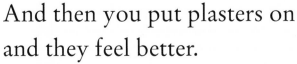

SCHOOL→

If you are a Teacher,
first you need to find some kids
and make them all come to your School
and Behave.
(Which means not talk unless you say so.)

And they are your Students.

Teachers MUST know all the answers
and how to be NOT BORING.

When your Students are sitting down,
you say, "Listen up! I'm the Teacher!
And I know EVERYTHING!"
Then you give them Projects
and teach them how to learn.

HERE'S WHAT ELSE
YOU GIVE THEM:
● Hard homework
★ Stars (I have ZILLIONS!)
● Breaks
✓ Rules and Toilet
   Behaviour (like "Use
   your listening ears!",
"Sit up straight!" and
"Toilet Paper goes IN
   the toilet!")

MY CHAIR

THE TOILET

If you are a Mummy or a Daddy
first you get some children.

(If you don't have any,
you can practice on your dolls,
or your cat
or your baby brother.)

Then you put them in pushchairs
and push them around.

You MUST be good at changing nappies
and not throw up.

HERE'S WHAT ELSE YOU MUST BE GOOD AT:

- Talking to Teachers

- Liking your children more than other people like them

- Protecting your children from hot food, sunburn and Other Dangers

- Tying shoelaces

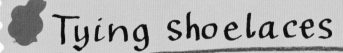

There are LOADS of other interesting jobs.
Like you could be a Police Officer
and arrest everyone.
Or you could be a Judge
and bang a hammer and go around
deciding things.

You could be a Waitress
and be Friendly and carry food on a tray.

You could be someone who helps people.
Like you could be a Vet
and help a bird.

You could be VERY smart
and know all about EVERYTHING
and write a book called
*How to Know EVERYTHING,
by Me, the Genius.*

If you practice EVERY day
and get VERY good at reading out loud
you could one day
maybe
become a Babysitter.

When you have chosen your Perfect Job,
you need to Get Employed.

First, you must write down EVERY SINGLE THING
you're good at on ONE PIECE OF PAPER
that's called your CV.

My CV

I am good at

every

(Sometimes it's SO HARD
to fit everything on only
one page, you just have to
use FIVE.)

single thing signed The Boss, Me

And then you have to keep showing it
to everyone.
"Look, Everyone!" you say.
"See how ABSOLUTELY marvellous I am?"

You must always bring your CV when you are trying to get the job.

HERE'S WHAT YOU SHOULDN'T BRING:
- [ ] Your whole family
- [ ] Your gerbils

WHEN YOU GET THERE YOU MUST:

Knock on the door

Walk in

Say your name (so they know it's you) and "How Do you Do" (which is office language and means "Hello," basically)

Shake hands

Sit down in a chair

Now you have a "Job Interview."
Which is when The Boss asks you TONS of questions
to find stuff out.
Like, are you a Criminal, for example.

My CV
Interests
Penguins
Gerbils
eating
Biscuits
Burping
Pooping
Sleeping

Thank you

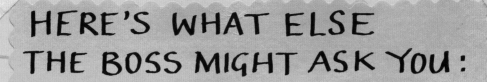

HERE'S WHAT ELSE THE BOSS MIGHT ASK YOU:

Can you read and write?

Do you know how to use scissors?

Can you dress yourself?

What time is it?

You shouldn't EVER bite the
Boss when he is talking to you.
Or sit in his lap.
Or fall asleep.

my CV

You must ALWAYS be on Your Best Behaviour.
(Except if you're getting a job as a Horrible Monster,
and then you HAVE to be HORRIBLE.)

At the end of the Interview you say,
"Please may I have the job?"
And The Boss says, "OK, here it is."

And that's when you shake hands again.
And shout, "Hooray for ME! I got the job!
I'm so COMPLETELY GREAT!"

And that's how you get a Job.

Now, basically, you say things like
"I'll take care of it!"
and "Sorry, I can't play Dollies tomorrow,
I have a JOB!"

And after a LONG TIME
if you're VERY good at the job,
and you work REALLY hard,
and you don't bite anyone,
you could actually
become The Boss.
(Like me.)

Sleep Expert

Moose Decorator

Masters of Disguise

Hairdresser

Boot Explorers

Butterfly Keeper

Dinosaur Artist

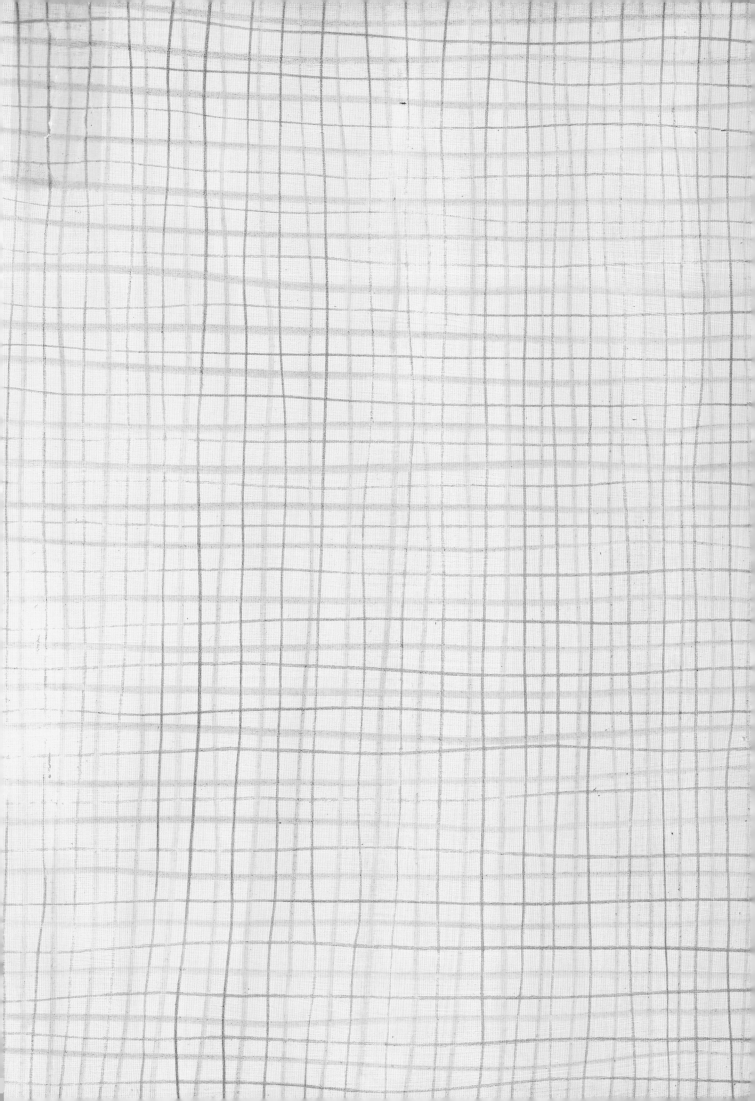

Also by Sally Lloyd-Jones and Sue Heap

ISBN 978-1-4063-2597-3

ISBN 978-1-4063-2333-7

Other books by Sue Heap

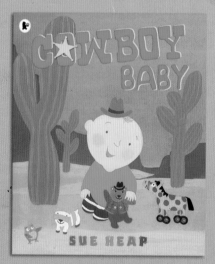

ISBN 978-1-4063-3064-9

Available from all good booksellers

www.walker.co.uk